IMAGES
of America

HOUSTON COUNTY
THE FIRST 100 YEARS

Namesake of Houston County, George Smith Houston was a well-respected and popular Alabama statesman of the 19th century. In 1841, at the age of 30, Houston was elected to the first of nine terms in the United States Congress. George S. Houston served as governor of Alabama from 1874 to 1878. He was re-elected to the U.S. Senate in 1878 and served until his death on December 31, 1879. Twenty-six years later, the state's 67th and last county to be created, was named in his honor.

IMAGES
of America

HOUSTON COUNTY
THE FIRST 100 YEARS

Dothan Landmarks Foundation, Inc.

ARCADIA
PUBLISHING

Published by Arcadia Publishing
Charleston, South Carolina

Library of Congress Catalog Card Number: 2003106493

For all general information contact Arcadia Publishing at:
Telephone 843-853-2070
Fax 843-853-0044
E-mail sales@arcadiapublishing.com
For customer service and orders:
Toll-Free 1-888-313-2665

Visit us on the Internet at www.arcadiapublishing.com

This book is dedicated to the citizens of Houston County, past and present, whose pioneering spirit, determination and faith make this a wonderful place to live.

CONTENTS

ACKNOWLEDGMENTS

Houston County: The First 100 Years was compiled as one of our organization's contributions to the celebration of Houston County's Centennial during 2003. For nearly a year, a small committee of volunteers graciously donated their time and talents to help make this book a reality. I would like to thank committee members Lewis Covington, T. Larry Smith, Dr. Martin Olliff, and Glois Speigner for all of their hard work and willingness to serve on this committee.

Most of the pictures in this publication were selected from photos in our archives. These images were collected or duplicated over the last 20 years from numerous individuals and organizations who supported our efforts to preserve the history of Houston County. A large number of these images were collected during the summers of 1994–1997 during our "Houston County History Project." This project, through the support of the Houston County Commission, enabled us to gather both photos and oral histories pertaining to life in the county. To all those individuals who graciously shared photos and their stories with us over the years, we sincerely appreciate your participation.

Other photos were collected over the last several months as this project took shape. While many came from private collections, we also have utilized photos from other institutions. Houston-Love Memorial Library, Auburn University, Alabama Department of Archives and History, Archives of Wiregrass History and Culture, Alabama Forestry Commission, and the Birmingham Public Library were all ready to assist us when asked. A special thanks is due to committee member Dr. Martin Olliff, director of Troy State Dothan's Archives of Wiregrass History and Culture. His expertise and contributions to this project have been invaluable.

And last but not least, I want to thank Katie White at Arcadia Publishing for including this book in their popular *Images of America* series.

While this book is not intended as a comprehensive history of Houston County, I hope it helps capture the spirit of our first 100 years. Landmark Park continues to collect historic photos of our past. If you have photos of Houston County or the surrounding area that you would like to preserve for future generations, please feel free to contact me.

William Holman
Executive Director
Dothan Landmarks Foundation
334-794-3452

INTRODUCTION

Houston County was officially created on February 9, 1903, as Alabama's last county to be formed, number 67. The new county was named by the legislature in honor of Alabama statesman, Gov. George Smith Houston of Limestone County. Seventy-two percent of Houston County's land area was carved from old Henry County with the remainder taken from both Geneva and Dale Counties. The little area of Alabama that became Houston County was already a prosperous section before countyhood. The area abounded in natural resources. The vast acreage of timber lands had stimulated a thriving economy based on naval stores and saw milling. The county was ready for the transition from a timber economy to an even more prosperous agricultural economy. With close to 18,000 people in the new county, the new economy flourished in the midst of fertile and highly cultivated land and the progressive, forward-looking urban communities with hundreds of large and small businesses and industries providing jobs for the people. An active retail sector attracted shopping from three states. Houston County borders the Chattahoochee River and Georgia on the east, Henry County on the north, Dale and Geneva Counties on the west, and Florida on the south. Dothan, once the largest town in Henry County, became the seat of the newly formed county.

One hundred years after the county's formation, Houston County has become a leading county in the state and "Hub of the Wiregrass Region" as the economic powerhouse. The area is known as a medical service provider and an educational and social center for over 500,000 tri-state and Wiregrass citizens. Houston County is now Southeast Alabama's largest county with over 89,000 people. Once covered in longleaf pine and wiregrass, Houston County's future is bright for the new Millennium. Many residents say, "As Dothan and Houston County goes; so goes the Wiregrass Region." Houston County's vast history has successfully led the county and her people to the brink of the 21st century with a positive attitude that the next 100 years will be even brighter.

One

ROOTS

Large herds of livestock like sheep, hogs, and especially cattle, were once found grazing the open range of Houston County. Spanish explorers, Native Americans, and early settlers all found the open "piney woods" perfect for livestock production.

The piney woods, which once stretched from Texas to the Carolinas, is one of North America's most biologically rich natural areas. Known as a wiregrass/longleaf pine habitat, this unique natural feature once consisted of approximately 97 million acres, but is now practically extinct. Even though the low-growing wiregrass plant was once widespread over many states, only the immediate area of Houston County has been referred to as the "Wiregrass Region."

The wiregrass/longleaf pine habitat is a fire-dependent ecosystem. For thousands of years, nature maintained this habitat with periodic summer wildfires caused by lightning strikes. Without fire, wiregrass will not reproduce and other trees will eventually shade out the pines. To maintain a longleaf pine/wiregrass habitat today, it must be periodically burned, as shown in this photograph.

When Spanish explorers arrived in the 1500s, they found Native Americans living along the banks of streams and rivers. Signs of these and other early inhabitants are still found in the form of Indian mounds and artifacts, including pottery shards and points (arrowheads.) This image is of the mural located at Dothan's Poplar Head Park on East Main Street.

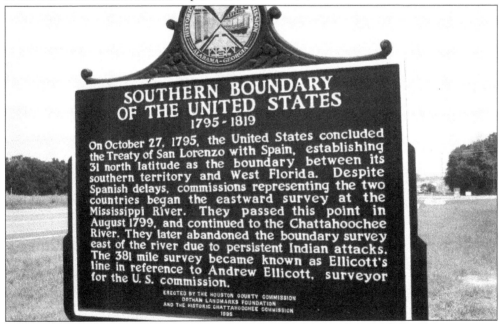

The historic marker located on U.S. 231 near the Florida state line marks an important part of Houston County's history. At one time, when Florida was Spain's possession, the southern boundary of what is now Houston County also served as the southern boundary of the United States. The line separating the two countries was surveyed in 1799 by Andrew Ellicott and is known as "Ellicott's Line."

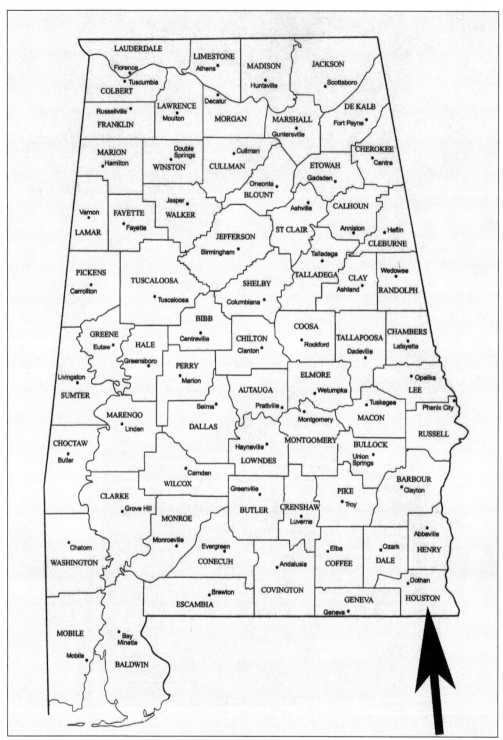

This modern-day map of Alabama shows all 67 counties, with Houston County depicted in the very southeastern corner. Houston County is the youngest of all Alabama counties and was created in 1903.

12

HOUSTON COUNTY

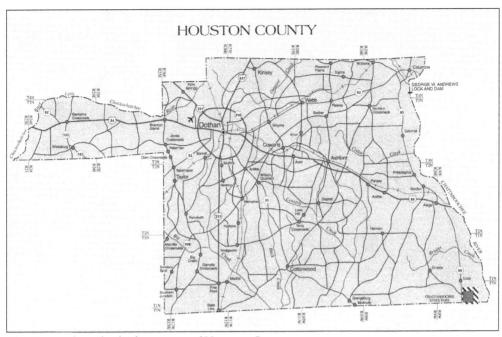

This is a modern-day highway map of Houston County.

As many of the longleaf pine in the Carolinas were harvested or died, many turpentine operations moved south into Alabama and Georgia looking for new tracts of land. This photo shows a turpentine worker cutting a "streak" into the trunk of a tree. This created an area where the pine resin could flow into cups to be collected. Often the resulting scar on the tree was referred to as a "face" or "catface."

Early settlers were attracted to the region because of the naval stores industry. This industry collected resin from the longleaf pine and distilled it into useful products such as pitch, tar, rosin, and spirits of turpentine. Pitch and tar were necessary products for caulking and waterproofing wooden ships. This photo shows a worker gathering resin to be carried back to the turpentine still for processing.

A typical crop of trees often included 10,000 faces. It was not uncommon for a turpentine still operator to lease or own several crops of longleaf pine.

Numerous turpentine stills once dotted the landscape of Houston County. These stills reduced producers' shipping cost by refining—and thus lightening—the crude product before it was hauled to market. This 1901 photo shows a turpentine still in Ashford.

Steamboats were once a common sight in Houston County, especially along the Chattahoochee River. Between 1828 and 1939, over 200 side and stern wheel riverboats regularly plied the river between the two towns of Columbus, Georgia, and Apalachicola, Florida. Stopping at any number of landings along the way, the boats carried cotton bales and barrels of turpentine downriver and returned with manufactured goods, food, and passengers.

Since rivers were the first "highways," it was natural that Houston County's oldest communities developed along the banks of the Chattahoochee River or major streams. Columbia and Gordon are two such examples. Pictured above is an early street scene in Columbia.

With the abundance of trees in the area, logging and sawmill operations also sprang up in the late 19th century. One such facility was that of Mr. Sidney Willoughby (pictured fourth from left). The bustling operation was located at Crosby, a small community southwest of Gordon.

Oxen were often used in sawmill operations, both in hauling logs out of the forests and in delivering heavy loads of lumber. This picture is believed to have been taken in Webb in the early 1900s.

For many early settlers, there was no electricity, no running water, no plumbing, and only a couple of young steers to pull the wagon.

Travel between towns was primitive in the early days. Except by railroad or steamboat, travel was difficult, slow, and time consuming. The fast-growing population of the southern part of Henry County—especially around Dothan—and the distance to the county seat in Abbeville led to a separation movement in 1900. This movement eventually led to the division of Henry County. Pictured is Will Armstrong of Columbia.

Shown here is the first Alabama Midland Railroad locomotive to enter what is now Houston County in 1889. Engineer was George Weatherford. This was engine number two, which was used in building the railroad from Bainbridge, Georgia, to Dothan and on to Montgomery. The introduction of the railroad brought increased trade, settlers, and industry to Houston County.

Once commercial fertilizer was introduced, Houston County's sandy soil became perfect for growing cotton. It quickly became the area's primary cash crop. The lone man, attired in his "Sunday-go-to-meeting" clothes and surveying the cotton bales, represents the many hopes placed in the cotton crop. For some in Houston County, their dreams of riches were dashed when the boll weevil struck its heavy blow.

Alabama's youngest county completed its first courthouse in 1905, just two short years after the county was formed from portions of Dale, Geneva, and Henry Counties. The new structure cost approximately $45,000. This courthouse stood until replaced in 1962.

Thomas M. Espy, Robert J. Reynolds, and George H. Malone (shown here) were the driving force for the creation of Houston County. These Henry County delegates convinced the 1901 Alabama Constitutional Convention to allow for the creation of a new county consisting of less 600 square miles. Many residents considered Malone the "Father of Houston County."

Shown below is the Columbia Public School in 1921. This was the old Henry County branch courthouse that was located in Columbia from 1889 to 1903, when Columbia became part of the new county of Houston. The courthouse building became a public school in 1903.

Two

EARNING A LIVING

The McDaniel brothers, Grady and Coly of Ashford, were quite proud of their store in the early 1900s. The establishment offered the *Capitol Clothing* and *Walk Over* shoe line. The brothers appear to be modeling their clothing lines in this photograph.

Benjamin Albert Forrester was the second state senator to serve Houston County. From Cowarts, he was the first to be elected, in 1906, and took his seat the following year. William Oates Long of Abbeville was the first senator in the new 35th District in 1903. Long was elected in Henry County in 1902 and served both counties until 1907.

Charles E. Walker and wife, Lillie Grice Walker, are shown in this photograph. He was a mayor of Columbia and first sheriff of Houston County. After the creation of Houston County, he was appointed sheriff by Governor Jelkes in 1903. He died before his term was over and N.B. Crawford was appointed sheriff until the next election. Mrs. Walker was Dothan's second librarian.

People of Houston County have always made the most of what they had. This image of a street scene in Columbia shows a yoke of oxen pulling a wagon. Note the handmade wagon body and top.

Dothan's Houston Hotel in 1960 was proud of its staff, especially its bellmen, who left good impressions on guests. Shown from left to right are Ben Jackson, Will ?, unidentified, and Jay Grayson.

This crowd of early Dothan citizens posed for their photo c. 1910, prior to a drawing to give away merchandise to lucky ticket holders. This practice was an early lottery used by merchants to attract business. Sanders Brothers & Co. was located on East Main Street and was a favorite hangout for local men to gossip and spin yarns. The owners were W.D. Sanders, John Sanders, and James Sanders, sons of J.G. Sanders.

J. Charles Thomas, who owned a store in Kinsey, would pack his REO truck in 1920 and deliver goods to area farmers in the county. This photo, taken in the winter, shows that Mr. Thomas was probably quite cold since his truck appears not to be equipped with a door.

The drugstore in Columbia around 1900 provided its customers with many creature comforts of the day. A cooling fan from the high ceiling, a soda fountain for refreshments, chairs for relaxing, a clock to determine time, as well as vast array of advertising all worked to entice people to spend money in the store.

Around 1916, W.M. Lewis and his associates stopped their hard work in the Lewis Tin Shop in Dothan to pose for this picture. Note the utensils and objects hanging from the shop's ceiling.

George Craft's *Peckerwood* sawmill was located on Fortner Street extension near Earline road in

Dothan around 1928. The small boy is Denvard Snell, Mr. Craft's grandson.

The E.R. Porter Hardware Co. on East Main Street is Dothan's oldest business and is Alabama's oldest operating hardware store. Mr. Porter came to Dothan from Troy, Alabama, and served as Dothan's first volunteer fire chief.

Mules and horses were once a vital commodity to Houston County residents. Pictured in front of Oscar M. Holman's livery stable in Ashford in the early 1900s, from left to right, are Judge Bruner, Lester Radney, Pat Garrett, Champion Bivens, Leroy Buckalt, Ed Pate, Reverend Stough, Leonard Jones, Byron Braswell, O.M. Holman, D.H. Knowles, Sid Williams, Dr. Walter Pate, Lester Fellows, and Lige Meadows.

Charles Walter Rainey posed for this photo in 1909. Rainey, a 1902 graduate of Georgia Tech, was Dothan's first professional engineer. He was superintendent of Dothan's first power generating plant.

Charles Rainey and an assistant worked at the Dothan Power Plant generator to keep the young city provided with power to meet its growing demands.

Due to the large number of wooden frame buildings and the use of wood or coal fired stoves and fireplaces, fire was a constant threat to Houston County residents. This horse-drawn fire wagon is shown racing to a fire in Dothan. Early Dothan fires were fought by volunteers until about 1903 when the city established a permanent fire department to combat the increasingly frequent fires.

The Dothan Fire Department in the 1940s was just as proud an institution as it is today. From left to right, Foy Glass, Ralph Franklin, Clyde Jewel, and Esto Pybus look sharp in their fresh uniforms. The photograph was taken on St. Andrews Street with the Dothan Opera House prominently viewed in the back left.

When railroads were first established in the Wiregrass, they created stations approximately every seven miles. The Taylor train depot in the 1920s was not large, but its office was distinguished and its staff dress was fairly formal. Note the ink wells and typewriters that aided the staff in its various tasks.

This image from the late 1940s or early 1950s shows the Central of Georgia depot staff in Dothan. Pictured from left to right are Ed Ransom, unidentified, ? Pruitt, Macon Childs, C.C. Bennett, Winston Griggs, unidentified, and Audrell Odum.

This Baldwin train was one of several that traveled along the Atlantic Coastline Railroad in Houston and Henry County for many years. Pictured are John Doby Dinkins and his sons—Tom, Jay, and Brad—who also worked on the train.

The Alabama, Florida, and Gulf Railroad was a shortline train that made runs from Cowarts to Greenwood, Florida. Sid Wilson owned the train. This 1935 photo of engine 14 captures a time when trains were an integral part of life.

The desire for a refreshing cola is timeless, but the trucks that delivered the sodas certainly changed as time went on. Note the chain-drive and solid-rubber tires on the REO truck parked at the edge of the First National Bank building in Dothan in this 1920 photo.

It was supreme ice cream. Supreme Meadow Gold Ice Cream, located in Dothan, was for more than a half century a recognized leader in the dairy industry. This group of employees was delighted to promote the company's new product line, Zooper Dooper. The ice cream plant located on East Powell Street grew from serving a small local community to providing ice cream throughout several states.

A combination of good soil, fertilizer, adequate rainfall, hard work, and faith produced many successful peanut crops in the area. Although this proud farmer's identity is unknown, his pose in the peanut field was a common sight in Houston County. He and his peers provided the area's economic base through their will to triumph over adversities common to farmers worldwide.

A strong back and a good team of mules were required to plow a field of peanuts. In the background, field hands can be seen shaking and stacking the peanuts around poles in the field to dry.

With cotton yields having succumbed to the boll weevil around 1915, area farmers gravitated towards the production of peanuts. The goober, as the peanut was called, proved to be a successful source of livelihood. Prior to the advent of modern-day peanut dryers, farmers stacked their peanuts in the field for about a month to dry before they were picked from the vine.

Once the peanuts were dry, the stack was hauled by mules to a stationary mechanical picker set up in the field to remove the peanuts from the vine. This farmer is attaching a chain from the handmade sled he is standing on to the pole in the center of the peanut stack. Once connected, the mules will topple the stack and drag it to the picker.

The Western Union office in Dothan was a busy place in the early 1900s. Employees certainly had to pause for this photograph. Western Union opened its office in Dothan about 1900. As telephones became a common fixture in many offices and homes, the telegraph lost some of its prominence. However, the telegram for many years remained the quickest way of transmitting news.

Young John William Baughman II, pictured in the lower left corner, was a carrier for *The Dothan Eagle* about 1922. The photo was made in the press room of the newspaper when it was located on Troy Street. Others pictured, from left to right, are S.T. Hall, Earnest Jackson, H.T. McKinnon, Dan Willis, E. Cody Hall, and Jim Harris.

A feed and seed store was as important to a local farmer as a supply of nuts to a squirrel. These attendants at the store transported hundreds of pounds of feed and seed each day. The feed was loaded on wagons and trucks to make sure crops were planted and farm animals fed.

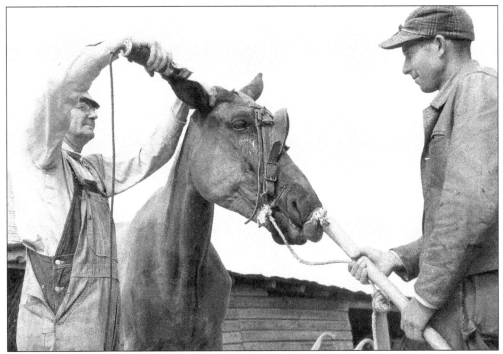

This photo shows W.M. Smith of Webb trimming the hair or "clipping" a mule belonging to Carlton Deese, also of Webb. When the photo was taken Mr. Smith was quoted as saying, "Most mules do not mind being clipped until I start using the clippers on the head, especially around the ears." Mr. Deese is using a twitch to help hold the mule still.

There were no air conditioned tractors in the mid-20th century when this farmer plowed his peanuts. Farmers took pride in their work and their harvest. There was knowledge that hard work meant the source of livelihood for a worker and his family.

At one time, Houston County was home of the second largest used farm equipment auction in the nation. Jones Farm Equipment Company, owned by the late Max Jones, operated for decades at the corner of Dothan's Ross Clark Circle and Highway 231 North. It was a hotbed of activity two days each month when farmers, dealers, and others from across the United States and abroad gathered to buy or sell used farm equipment.

For decades, Dr. Coy Poitevint provided the area with much-needed veterinary care. His animal hospital on South Oates Street in Dothan responded to the call of sick pets or farm animals.

If you needed a new Ford car or truck in 1926, you had to travel no further than the Malone Motor Company in Dothan. There were few choices in models or colors. Henry Ford had decreed that "customers could buy one of his cars in any color they wanted, as long as it was black."

Houston County once claimed two towns with the name Ardilla—one now in the city limits of Dothan, and the other near Gordon, where this jail once stood. The latter Ardilla eventually vanished after W.S. Wilson's sawmill operation burned and was moved to Malone, Florida. Pictured at the Ardilla jail, from left to right, are Dan Battle, Jeff Newman, Jesse Hall, Little John Brown, two unidentified people, Herman Hardwick, "Lightning Bug," "Fancy John" Brown, and Frank Williams.

Dothan's finest has always been a source of pride for the city, and the distinguished group of officers and city officials in this late 19th century photograph was no exception.

Farm produce has long been a source of income for Houston County farmers. This late 1940s image shows assistant county farm agent Clark Rudder talking with C.W. Kirkland of Webb about his watermelon crop.

It was usually a cold winter day when people gathered for "hog killing." The hogs were butchered and the pork was secured in a smoke house or, in later years, a freezer locker. In 1945 Ray Smith butchered these hogs in the yard of Ivy Simmons on Ruth Street in Dothan.

Employees of the F.W. Woolworth store in Dothan gathered for this photo in the late 1920s or early 1930s. Woolworth's was a popular business in downtown Dothan until it closed in December of 1983.

Another popular Dothan business was the S.H. Kress & Co. store, which stood on the corner of South Foster and East Main. Like many downtown businesses, the store flourished until the era of malls and giant discount stores.

Three

MAIN STREET AND FRONT PORCHES

The Houston National Bank was one of the many businesses that became a victim of the Great Depression. It closed in 1931. The bank building remained a landmark and continued to occupy the corner of Main and St. Andrews Street in Dothan into the late 20th century. No traffic lights were needed when this photograph was made and a simple small sign directed traffic to "keep to the right."

The streets of Dothan were hot on August 24, 1902, but the town's citizens were dressed in full hats, suits, and white dresses that clipped the dirt streets. Please note the telegraph wires that crossed the street at the top of the photo.

The Hammond and Young Drug Store, located at the corner of Main and Foster Streets in Dothan, was the center of activity for the town at the turn of the 20th century. The bell tower in the upper left of the photo marks the building in which the Dothan City Council met between 1889 and 1904.

When this photograph was taken, Cottonwood was in a time of transition. Some traveled by the new mode of transportation, the car, while a horse and buggy seemed more practical to others. The words "Welcome to Cottonwood" were stretched across the street for all.

There were more cars in downtown Columbia by the mid-1920s. However, the new machines could not replace a good wagon and team of horses. The cars could not haul goods like the wagon and the horses did not run out of gas or have flat tires.

When construction began in 1906 on this Dothan building, it was designed to serve as a warehouse. The building was finished as the Hotel Martin by Dan and Buck Baker. The wedge-shaped building on East Main offered respite for several decades to weary travelers and drummers visiting Dothan to sell their goods.

SCENE IN THE LOBBY OF HOTEL MARTIN

212 EAST MAIN STREET — DOTHAN, ALA.   D-4292

The lobby of the Hotel Martin appears somewhat stark by today's standards. The hotel, which opened around 1908, sustained a steady flow of guests and visitors for decades. Located on the south side of East Main Street, the narrow, wedge-shaped building survived long after its builders, the Baker brothers.

This photograph, from the later 1930s or early 1940s, shows Mr. Sam Hall's store building on Main Street in Gordon. Mr. Hall is believed to be the gentleman sitting on the bench with a white shirt and hat. The other people pictured are unidentified.

In Columbia, Model T's and Tin Lizzies of the early 20th century had no paved roads on which to travel. The town did offer respite from the farm by providing stores where goods could be purchased and the opportunity to visit with others. Notice the statue, called "Sally," and water pool in the center of the street.

It was parade day in Dothan when this group lined the streets in the 1940s. The Dothan Charities Chest was a forerunner of The United Way. The black gentleman with hat in hand signaled his observation of the day by wearing new bib overalls. This was a time to wear your Sunday best and enjoy the occasion.

In Columbia, the oxen teamed together by a yoke were probably more comfortable than the people shown in this July 4, 1906 photograph. The oxen were in the shade while Columbia residents braved the hot sun for speeches and revelry commemorating the holiday.

A man in the early 20th century was not properly dressed without his hat. These gentlemen posing on a Dothan street were also aware that a vest, bow tie, and watch fob added to a man's complete ensemble.

Like all drug stores, Wright's Drug Store in Ashford was a popular place for city residents. Wright Drug Company was established by Reuben D. Wright in 1919. The store is shown in this 1920s photo.

In the 1940s, looking east from the intersection of Oates and Main Street in Dothan one could see the main entrance of the Houston County Courthouse; the Martin-Davis Theater, which was the area's premier movie palace; and part of what is now the Downtown Historic District. Interestingly, the restrooms that served the courthouse were located across the alley from the building and were connected to neither sewer nor septic systems.

This is perhaps the earliest photo of downtown Dothan in the early 1890s. The two-story brick building pictured on East Main was Dothan's first such structure and was owned by Dr. James A. Balkum. Dr. Balkum was an early Dothan pioneer, developer, and city commissioner. This structure housed retail stores on the first floor and the Silver Hotel upstairs. Later, the building was purchased by the Blumberg family as the first permanent location for their department store.

Construction of the U.S. Courthouse and Post Office in Dothan was nearing completion in January 1911 when this photo was made. Built at a cost of $85,000, the structure still stands on the corner of Troy and North Foster Street.

The U.S. Courthouse and Post Office, also known as the Federal Building, is an excellent example of governmental architecture during the early years of the 20th century. The building, completed in the Classic Revival style, served as a courthouse and post office until the new post office was constructed in 1964. At present, the structure serves as a courthouse and federal office building and is listed on the National Register of Historic Places.

Pictured here is the interior view of the U.S. Courthouse and Post Office shortly after opening. The sign on the counter reads "Warning—all persons are warned against throwing ink, spitting on the floor or walls, or otherwise defacing this building—violators will be prosecuted."

The Rogers' farmhouse, located near the railroad tracks at William's Station near Columbia, conveys much of the architecture of the early 1900s. The many windows allowed cool cross-ventilation to sweep across the high ceilings. The high-pitched roof insured water and debris would be swept away. The swing and chairs on the porch marked the family's welcome for visitors. This home has been fully renovated.

This photo of the J.B. Taylor home on Washington Street in Columbia was taken December 13, 1934. The house, built in 1845, had survived hard weather, the Civil War, and much living by the time this image was taken.

The Thrasher House, on the corner of North Foster and West Adams Street in Dothan, opened in 1891 for tired, hungry drummers, or salesmen, to sleep and eat. The food was good and there was no charge for drummers' wives. This fine group posed for the camera in the 1900s.

This *c.* 1940 photo shows the Sam Bowdon home in Gordon. Mr. Bowdon was one of Gordon's most prosperous merchants and plantation owners after the Civil War. The home was torn down in the 1960s.

J.W. Baughman, a local builder of considerable renown in the early 20th century, constructed this house in Dothan in 1892. Mr. Baughman built numerous residential and commercial buildings in the area.

The Baughman family later moved into this home located at 409 East Main Street. It remained for decades until time, progress, and city growth caused its demise.

The Sidney Willoughby home, built in 1908 with lumber from his sawmill, still stands in the Crosby Community south of Gordon. C. Yates Willoughby, Sidney's son, lived here and operated the family plantation. Barton Willoughby, a grandson of Sidney, still operates the family farm.

This tenant farm house in Webb was improved under the auspices of the Alabama Cooperative Extension Service. Tin replaced the roof's wooden shingles and bricks replace rocks for the chimney. A new coat of paint completed the renovation.

Many of the beautiful old homes that once graced Dothan streets have long been torn down in the name of progress. These homes were once located along the north side of West Main Street c. 1910. The three homes pictured, from left to right, were owned by P.N. Spann, M.S. Spann, and the Brown family.

This photograph, taken in 1910, is of the Sam Davis family in front of their home in Wicksburg. Pictured, from left to right, are the following: (front row) daughters Mert, Minnie Pearl, Metha, and Beth (seated holding a doll); (back row) George Davis, Lon Holland, Sam Davis, and Fanny Davis.

Thomas White and his family posed for this picture in 1910 in front of their house, now located on the Old Headland Highway. The house was on the east side of the road just north of the cypress pond. Pictured, from left to right, are Nannie, Gussie, Cora, Myrtle, Maggie (Green), Thomas V., Thomas Edgar, Foy, and Walter.

The open hallway or "dogtrot," which ran through the center of this house, was once a common feature of homes in Houston County. This 1912 photograph is of the Pearson home, which once stood near Highway 231 South approximately one mile from the Dothan city limits. Pictured, from left to right, are Agnes Pearson Harris, E.D. Pearson, Eddie Elizabeth Merritt Pearson, Oscar Pearson, Vera Pearson, Dottie Pearson, Marguerite Nordon Lott, and unidentified.

The M.S. Spann home on West Main Street in Dothan shows the rewards of economic opportunity in Houston County. The Spann family members were early entrepreneurs in the area.

The Mays Hotel in Columbia stood on the south side of courthouse square. Later, Dr. John Fletcher Yarborough, who developed the cure for pellagra, bought the hotel for his first hospital. When it burned, he built another hospital in Columbia. (See page 80.)

Family has always been important to the people of Houston County. Three generations of the Williams had their picture taken on the steps of their home in this undated photograph. The home was on what is now Westgate Parkway in Dothan.

Gingerbread trim and fish scale siding decorate the 1895 W.C. Pilcher home. Mrs. Pilcher and daughter Lula pose on the porch while son Louie drapes himself over the gate of the picket fence. The home was located on South Saint Andrews Street in Dothan.

Dr. and Mrs. Clarence Lee Conner Atkinson raised their family in this home on North Main Street in Columbia. Two sons would go on to become United States Navy admirals. Dr. Atkinson kept an office in the rear of Columbia's City Drug Store.

The rural family pictured above was updating their home when this photograph was taken. The members covered the original log cabin with ship-lap and board-and-batten siding, and put in new roof shingles. Note the extensive split rail fence and the mud-and-stick chimney of the structure behind the front house.

The three-quarter porch on this family's home was common in rural Houston County. The fence is made from "scrap" boards sawn from local lumber. This photograph was taken in the 1890s.

A distinguishing characteristic of this home is the five-cornered, two-story bay window. The window has obviously enlarged from its first iteration that had fit the gable above it. The picket fence is an excellent example of that architectural feature. Note the gazebo in the front yard and the hitching post for visitors' horses.

The Register family posed in front of their dogtrot log cabin and included in the photo one of the family's most important possessions—their mules. A family's livelihood often depended on owning or having access to a well-trained mule.

Most of the early homes in Gordon have long since disappeared. One early home that remains is the Vaughn-Tuttle home, built in 1854. The home was once occupied by Dr. Daniel Vaughn, an early Gordon physician. Most recently it was occupied by Mrs. Hoke Tomlinson, a former mayor of Gordon who passed away in 2003.

Originally built in 1894 as a hotel, the McArthur home was a longtime landmark in Ashford. This photo was taken in the 1920s when the home was located across from the railroad depot. This house was moved to Avon in 1988 and is currently undergoing renovation. (See photo on page 126.)

Although the porch is no longer attached, the George Craft home still stands on Fortner Street extension near Earline Road in Dothan. This family operated a sawmill near the same location (featured on the cover of this book and on pages 28–29). Denvard Snell is the small boy in middle of photo.

Four

MIND, BODY, AND SPIRIT

One of the few institutions of higher learning in southeast Alabama in the late 1800s was the Mallalieu Seminary in Kinsey. Supported by the Methodist Episcopal Church, the school taught grades 1 through 12 and offered courses such as Greek, algebra, Latin, history, chemistry, music, geology, and both New and Old Testaments. The school closed in 1923.

Builder J.W. Baughman leaned against the tall post to survey the progress of his project—the building of Howell School in Dothan 1902. After serving as an elementary school for four decades, then a sewing factory for several more, the building on East Newton Street still stands.

Students and teachers in all classes of the school in Pansey turned out for this photograph taken in 1935. The current and first woman lieutenant governor of Alabama, Lucy Baxley, is a native of Pansey.

Freshly scrubbed faces, clean starched clothes, and quiet children are ready for picture day. In the late 1800s, many Gordon school children did not wear shoes in warm weather.

The present Dothan High School on South Oates Street was completed in 1939. It replaced the former three-story brick school building of 1911, which was located on the site of the present Houston-Love Memorial Library. Dothan now has two public high schools. The second is Northview High School on U.S. Highway 431.

Young Junior High School was built in 1921 at the corner of Lafayette and Dusy Street in Dothan. Children came and left, teachers retired, but the building still stands.

Dothan's Highland Elementary School, constructed in 1924, is another early school still in use. Situated at the corner of Montana and West North Streets, the building is a magnet school today.

One lone, straight chair remained on the porch of Dupree School, located south of Ashford, when this picture was taken. The school is now closed but one is left to wonder if the chair was used for a student who did not act properly in class.

The children of Wicksburg in 1927 were glad to have a chance for school. Their teacher, Amanda Whitaker, and their principal, Metha Davis, were pleased to have them.

Mabel and Euffie Weems were the first graduates of Columbia Colored School in 1941. Needless to say, the girls were proud, but not nearly so proud as their family and friends.

PROGRAMME

Recital by the Musical Department
Houston County High School.

Chorus	Welcome Sweet Spring.	Rubinstein
	" Glee Club. ·	
Song	If I Built a World for You	Lehmann
	Miss Edyth Davis.	
Piano	Venetian Love Song	Nevin
	Miss Rosalie Skipper	
Duet	Ma Belle, Mignon	Field
	Misses Norma and Maria Bryan.	
Piano	By the Fountain	Bohm
	Miss Virginia Atkeson.	
Song	Over the Ocean Blue	Petrie
	Walter Oakley	
Duet	Lustpiel Overture	Bela
	Misses Skipper and McCann.	
Song	A Wispered Vow	Hartwell-Jones
	Alex Wood.	
Piano	Air de Ballet	Chaminade
	Miss Beryl McCann.	
Duet	Hark to the Eandolin.	Parker
	Misses Koerber and Clarke.	
Piano	L. Argentine	Ketterer
	Miss Myrtle Jones.	
Song	Carissima	Penn
	Miss Harrison.	
Chorus	Pond Lilies	Forman
	Glee Club	

The music department of Houston County High School worked hard on its recital. The 1909 program is indicative of the pride the school had for the arts.

Children and balloons are a natural combination. This c. 1923 image is of a "balloon party" held by Dothan's new Community Services Department at a park, located on the corner of Troy and North Foster. The large building in the background is the U.S. Courthouse and Post Office Building, often referred to as the Federal Building.

This image is of a group of Mallalieu Seminary students and faculty gathered in front of the girl's dormitory in 1917. One of the Kinsey school's most famous alumni is Robert Jones of Brannon Stand. He became the nationally known Dr. Bob Jones, famous fundamentalist evangelist who established Bob Jones University in Greenville, South Carolina.

Harmon School served the community southeast of Ashford. This 1916 photograph shows the class with its teacher, H.T. Scarborough, who is standing behind the crowd and wearing a necktie.

Flowers Chapel, west of Dothan, served as school and church for local residents. This photo was taken *c.* 1900.

Dr. Earl F. Moody (seated in center) founded Moody Hospital on North Alice Street in Dothan in 1913. He and his fellow physicians, pictured here in 1920, even made house calls. Pictured, from left to right, are the following: (front row) Dr. King, Dr. Hopkins, Dr. Moody, Dr. Green, and unidentified; (back row) Dr. Burdeshaw, Dr. Keyton, Dr. Hilson, Dr. Cannady; and Dr. Smith.

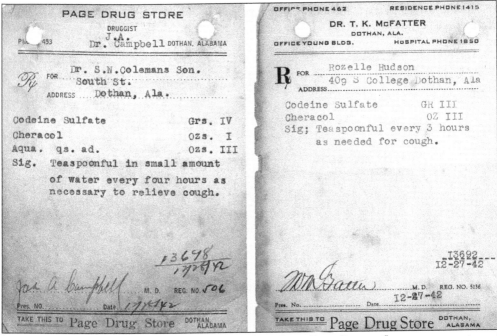

The names recorded on the old prescriptions from Page Drug Store reflect a cross-section of ...eople in Dothan in 1942. The standard ingredients for the cough medicine also reflect the ...mited medical technology of the day. Note that Dr. Campbell simply wrote his prescription ... Dr. S.N. Coleman's "son." Apparently codeine sulfate was a base for many medicines since ... was the first ingredient on both prescriptions.

The old Madrid School of the late 1800s was unpainted and had no glass windows or air-conditioning to blow cool breezes. The teachers did, however, teach all to read, write, and do arithmetic. Many students started school only after crops were harvested and others remained home if they were needed for chores.

The location of this school is unknown, but it was fortunate to have glass win
time, all the children, regardless of age, sat in one big room.

Dr. David V. Jemison is thought to be the county's first African-American dentist. Dr. Jemison practiced in Dothan during the mid-20th century. At the same time, Dr. William Russell Greenfield was the county's first African-American general practice physician.

The staff of Frazier-Ellis Hospital in Dothan had to be quite efficient to care for the needs of their patients with such a small group. In the 1920s, when this photo was made, some hospital stays were quite lengthy for procedures that are today performed on an out-patient basis. The gentleman in the center of photo is Dr. John T. Ellis and Dr. A.S. Frasier is standing on the far right.

Dr. F.G. Granger from Ashford served as Houston County's health officer during the 1930s. The era offered little technology to alleviate many illnesses like tuberculosis and typhoid fever, as well as to relieve unsanitary conditions, untreated water, and open ditches.

Although the battle of the mosquito is still being fought today, the war against the pest and its ever-carrying ability began years ago. This photo is of a WPA project to dig a drainage ditch near Cheshire Pond in the Enterprise community of Houston County.

Moody Hospital, located on North Alice Street in Dothan, opened in 1913. Years later, the hospital size was increased to the above size. It operated until around 1966 when it closed permanently. This hospital administered the first dose of penicillin in the state in 1949.

The Moody Hospital nurses in the mid-20th century were not only a caring group of women, but they were quite attractive. Notice the variety of uniforms depicting each one's degrees and qualifications.

The Dothan Opera House has seen many events during its century of existence. This group of nursing school graduates in the 1920s was just beginning careers that would lead them to area hospitals and the bedsides of the sick.

After first practicing medicine in Ashford, Dr. John Fletcher Yarborough built the Yarborough Sanitarium in Columbia in 1915. Having contracted the dreaded disease pellagra, he became intensely interested in patients with this ailment. Dr. Yarborough discovered a cure for this awful disease and quickly attracted the attention of the medical world. He later moved to Montgomery where he died in 1950 at the age of 86. (See page 61.)

Known as the Blumberg Home when Dr. Paul Flowers purchased the building in 1950, it quickly became known as Flowers Hospital. Expanded several times, it remained on West Main Street in Dothan until a fire in the 1970s.

Southeast Alabama General Hospital was dedicated on September 1, 1957, and began admitting patients on September 9. The hospital began with 33 physicians on medical staff, 70 beds, and 76 employees.

The Gordon Methodist Church was constructed in 1899, and is the only known building used by the congregation. The church began in 1885, perhaps meeting in a brush arbor or in local homes. This building still stands.

Columbia Baptist Church is the oldest Baptist church in Houston County, established in 1835. This photo shows the church as it appeared c. 1884. The first pastor and one of six founding members was Rev. Edmund Talbot, a notable Columbia pioneer.

The Columbia Presbyterian Church was organized in 1888 in Henry County by the Alfrod, Dunwoody, Beach, Purcell, and Brown families. In 2003, the congregation consists of a few members who lead their own services in lieu of a pastor.

The congregation of the Holy Church of Christ in Dothan appeared to be an austere group, possibly absorbed in their religion and their daily lives.

Although Jewish families had resided in Dothan since 1890, the only organized Jewish life consisted of irregular worship services held in local homes. In 1928, the Jewish community organized and formed Temple Emanuel the following year. This photo shows the Temple's new building shortly after construction in 1940 on North Park Avenue.

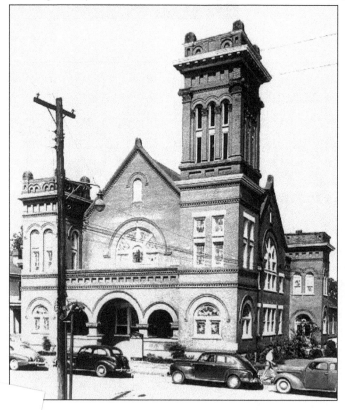

Foster Street Methodist Church in Dothan was an imposing structure. The church is the forerunner of what is today the First United Methodist Church on West Main Street.

African Americans in Houston County and the Wiregrass Region played a major role in the area's development. Religion and faith were made manifest in community churches such as the Colored Methodist Church built in 1877. In 1888, the church changed its name to Gaines Chapel and in 1910 to the current name—Cherry Street African Methodist Episcopal (AME) Church. It is believed to be the oldest AME church in the state of Alabama.

This photo of First Missionary Baptist Chruch in Dothan was taken in the 1940s. The pastor of the church, Rev. C.T. Hayes, is shown seated on the first row, the fifth person from the left.

Kinsey Methodist Church was first named Forrest Home in 1883. Pastors associated with this church were Morton, Hammitt, Thames, Robertson, Grant, Owens, Jones, Pooly, Dean, Mc-Durmont, Wilson, Baldwin, Brannon, Carlton, Northcutt, Daughtry, and Lewis, among others.

The First Missionary Baptist Church has long been a part of Dothan's religious community. First organized in 1889 as New Hope Baptist Church, it was later renamed the First Colored Church of Dothan and finally First Missionary Baptist. The church is listed on the Alabama Register of Landmarks and Heritage and is located on Chickasaw Street.

Five

GOOD TIMES

Woods Mill near Columbia was the scene of this bountiful Methodist picnic in 1905. It is thought that most of these people lived in Dothan. Some of the identified people are Ethel Nix, Frank Mullen, Lucile McClure, Mrs. Ed Nix, Mrs. S.E. Gellerstedt, Mrs. W.T. Jones, Carl Simenton, and Ben Grant.

This picture was made in 1896 during a picnic outing at the junction of the Chattahoochee River and Omussee Creek in Columbia. On right with umbrella and leaning against a tree is W.L. Lee. He is talking to Miss Ellen Thomas, whom he later married. This area is now Omussee Creek Park, a county-maintained facility with a picnic area and boat ramp.

Blewitt's Mill on Omussee Creek in Columbia was also a gathering place for young people. Pictured in this 1902 photograph, from left to right, are the following: (front row) Walt Bowden and Bert Myers; (back row) Clarkie Purcell Crapps, Thornie Beach, Fannie Thompson, Charlie Freeman, Annie Wood Bowden, Minnie Yarbrough, and Colbert McGriff.

This group of ladies and gentlemen were all too pleased to pose for the photographer in front of one of Dothan's first newspapers, *The Wiregrass Siftings*. Pictured driving the wagon is J.M. Smith while Hunter Armstrong is in the rear of the wagon. E.R. Porter is on the horse. The women in no particular order are Ida Miller, Orie Snead, Annie Dickinson, and Marilou Leslie.

This group gathered at the fish trap to enjoy a Thanksgiving Day outing at Blewitts Mill near Columbia in 1895. The gentleman in the center of the picture facing the camera is Samuel Murphy Dunwoody, who served in the state legislature and eventually became Alabama's commissioner of agriculture. He created Alabama's Agricultural Experiment Station system and is largely responsible for the selection of Headland as the state's first experiment station.

Fishing has always been a popular activity in Houston County. Pictured fishing at Bazemore's Mill Pond near Grangerburg is Mrs. Kitty Pate, wife of Doctor W.E. Pate Sr. Dr. Pate was one of Ashford's early doctors.

Dr. and Mrs. Pate's son, W.E. Pate Jr., inherited his mother's fishing abilities. Mr. Pate left the water's edge to fish from his boat on Bazemore's Mill Pond in the 1960s.

Head, Heart, Hands, Health (4-H) is the long-time youth education branch of the Cooperative Extension Service and was very popular among students in rural Houston County. In this photo, the Kinsey 4-H club marches in one of the 1950s Peanut Festival parades.

The statue "Sally," which once stood in the center of Main Street in Columbia, was a favorite gathering spot for years. The statue received its nickname from the Salmagundi Club, the women's club in Columbia that paid for its purchase. It was originally erected in front of the Henry County branch courthouse in Columbia.

The date of this photograph is not known. However, these boy scouts and the children seem to be enjoying this parade on North Foster Street in Dothan. The white building to the left is the Federal Building.

Dothan High School football players from the 1920s illustrate the long history of high-school sports and its importance to Houston County citizens. These "tough guys" outfitted themselves with leather helmets and thick clothing.

These men were too happy to race their horses in the Columbia, July 4, 1906 celebration. No track was needed—just the streets of downtown Columbia.

People in 1892 did not bicycle for exercise. It was a mode of transportation. Clarence Atkison, G.L. Radley, and John Duke enjoyed comparing notes on their Columbia travels.

Even John Philip Sousa would have been proud of the newly reorganized Dothan High Band of 1936. The black and red capes that had been recaptured from previous bands made a complete uniform, with identical pants and tops unnecessary for members. The insert is of Forrest Boyd, band director.

Patriotism has always been prevalent in Dothan. It was certainly magnified the day this gathering occurred on St. Andrews and East Main Street in the early 1920s. Although the bunting accented the day, the congregating of the people exemplified the spirit.

A boy and his bike go together like peaches and cream. Eight-year-old Karl Oakley of Columbia was certainly proud of his new bicycle in the 1890s. His attire was the Sunday dress of the day for young boys.

This group is enjoying a Sunday afternoon on the grounds of Columbia's old cotton factory. The woodpile supplied the plant with fuel. Just behind the trees on the right is the bluff over which Murrell's "blood thirsty" band of robbers reportedly would throw bodies of victims they had waylaid.

A young man sits proudly in his new cowboy outfit astride his horse. Although his hat is a bit large, his leopard-spot chaps fit perfectly.

This fellow from Taylor, c. 1890, was proud of his Masonic chapter. He wore his white apron, sash, and Masonic medallion with dignity.

History is replete with "big fish stories." Foy Chalker, W.R. Gordon, Toby Dove, and Red Dove of Dothan produced proof of their fish tales in this 1940 photograph.

A Saturday afternoon western movie was standard entertainment for much of America before the advent of television. Houston County was proud to claim Johnny Mack Brown, actor and western movie hero, in the 1930s, 1940s, and 1950s as a favorite son. Pictured with Brown, from left to right, are an unidentified person, Stancil King, and Frank Pridgen.

First Baptist Church of Dothan has always had a strong music program. Their concert orchestra under the direction of B.M. Cherry in 1940 added to the church's attraction.

The Owl Club of Columbia is pictured in the City Drug Store about 1898. This social club often gathered at the drug store for social activities. Officers were Wood Beach, president; Colbert McGriff, vice president; Lee McGriff, secretary; York McGriff, treasurer; and Y. Conner, ways and means.

Scouting has always been a popular activity in Houston County. Although the purpose of
this scout ceremony is unknown, it is believed to have taken place in Dothan in 1926. The
gentleman in the center of the photograph wearing a dark suit is Robert L. Gaines, president of
the Choctawhatchee Council of Scouts.

Although the women in this photograph are unidentified, athletic activities have long been
enjoyed by women in Houston County.

Originally called Fritter's Spring, Porter's Fairyland on Cowarts Road southeast of Dothan was a popular gathering place for people from all over the Wiregrass. The pavilion on the right contained a jukebox providing music to everyone from square dancers to Jitterbuggers. Named for entrepreneur E.R. Porter, the resort flourished between the late 1920s and the 1960s.

Kelly Springs in the northwest corner of the county provided the same recreational pleasures as Porter's Fairyland. During World War II, Kelly Springs drew airmen from nearby Napier Field as well as local residents and family reunions. The water there was notoriously cold—a "boiling spring" (artesian well) fed the pond. Kelly Springs flourished until Dothan began building public swimming pools in the 1960s.

Houston County Shriners held their own Alcazar parade until joining with the Peanut Festival parade. The ceremony was graced by floats like the one shown in this undated photo. Shriners support a network of 22 Shriner hospitals renowned for advanced treatment for young children.

A lucky group of boy scouts from Ashford traveled to the 1939 World's Fair in New York City in this bus. The group was chaperoned by the late Will Wright Sr.

You can do more with a book than just read it. With practice, you can learn to balance it on your head for good posture, as these girls did in one of Dothan's National Peanut Festival parades.

The streets in downtown Dothan were packed with people along the National Peanut Festival parade route in 1964 as the previous year's queen, Rosemary Shelton of Colquitt, Georgia, waved her goodbyes. The onlookers were lined five deep along the streets.

Gentlemen, start your engines—or your downhill glide in your "Cubmobile"—for the National Peanut Festival activities.

Smiles abound on parade day in Dothan. Even if you still have your curlers in your hair (as the girl in the right corner does), a smile takes precedence over hair.

The National Peanut Festival Midway in Dothan was a rather lonely site in the daytime.

The same midway came alive at night as area residents sought entertainment.

This young man sits atop a precursor to the modern moped in this undated photograph. Because motorcycles were less expensive than cars and faster than horses, mailmen in the early 1900s used them throughout Houston County. Motorcycling remains a popular sport in Houston County and the Wiregrass. Since its 2001 inauguration, the annual Dothan Bike Fest has drawn between 1,000 and 2,500 enthusiasts.

Plenty of good times have been held inside Dothan's Opera House on North and Andrews Streets. Dothan's mayor Buck Baker was the administrator largely responsible for the construction of the Opera House and City Hall, completed in 1915. This structure is now listed on the National Register of Historic Places.

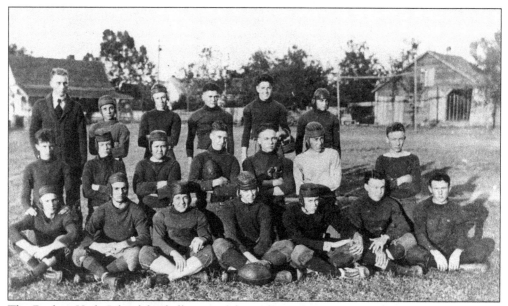

The Dothan High School football team of the early 1920s is shown in this picture. Hollywood movie star Johnny Mark is pictured standing second from right.

It doesn't snow in Houston County every year, but a thin blanket of the white, moist flakes provided Columbia kids Larry Oakley, Mike Zorn, and Mike Oakley a chance to practice their snowball making. The date of the happy day is unknown.

The 1975 National Peanut Festival Golf Tournament took place on October 18 and 19 at Olympia Spa, since renamed the Dothan National Country Club. Houston County's warm, sunny weather is ideal for a long golf season. Five public and private courses serve the county, which is home of the nationally-renowned Future Masters Tournament. The tournament was created by Press Thornton Sr. in 1950 for golfers 10 to 18 years old.

In 1919, Max Fortner built one of the first airplanes in Houston County from a kit. He received flying lessons from barnstormer E.P. Lott, who went on to become Eastern Airlines station manager in Chicago. Pictured, from left to right, are Etta Ennis, Mrs. Lott, Clara Moore Fortner, and Max Fortner.

Eastern Air Lines—The Great Silver Fleet—provided Dothan and Houston County with the area's first real commercial air traffic. The first airport (located where Westgate Park is situated today) moved to its present location in 1967 and Eastern Air Lines became a part of history's past.

Dothan's first airport terminal, located at what is now Westgate Park, was a welcome sight. This building, constructed in 1940, marked progress for the Wiregrass. The region finally had air transportation, connecting it to other rapidly-growing areas.

Six

AROUND THE COUNTY AND TODAY

Members of the Weems family, who owned a prosperous 200-acre farm in Columbia, had their photograph taken at Smith Grocery, *c.* 1953. Pictured, from left to right, are the following: Margaret Weems, Charlie Weems, William Weems White (child), Monroe 'Uncle Pike" Weems, Lige Weems, and Ruby Weems.

In 1962, Houston County replaced the 1905 courthouse with this modern building designed by local architect Joe Donofro. The façade of wire mesh provided a monolithic appearance fashionable in the era. It also shaded the offices within from the glaring sun.

The Dothan architectural firm of Wade McNamara & Parrish designed this postmodern courthouse to replace the outdated 1962 building. Delays plagued construction, resulting in lawsuits, as well as frustrated judges, workers, and county commissioners. The building opened in 2003.

Although situated in neighboring Dale County, the Dothan Regional Airport serves many Houston County travelers. The current airport evolved from Napier Field, a World War II aviation training base for American and Royal Air Force pilots. This "ultra-modern" terminal opened in 1967, with Southern Airways providing jet service to Atlanta and, beginning in 1968, to Washington, D.C. and New York City.

The Dothan Regional Airport expanded operations with the opening of its new 27,000-square-foot terminal in October 2002. Aviation and avionics companies occupy other buildings at the 1,200-acre facility, including Pemco World Air Services, FlightSafety International, Alabama Jet Center, and Flightline of Dothan.

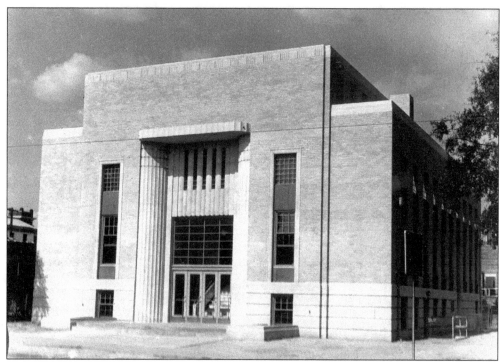

Built in 1938, as a project of the federal Works Progress Administration, this brick building was accentuated with beautiful marble just inside its door. It hardly appears to be the county's second jail. The county built a third jail in 1981 and renovated this edifice in 2000–2001 to house the Houston County Sheriff's Department.

Built during the administration of Sheriff Lamar Glover, the new Houston County Jail was occupied early in 2003. Earl Durden, owner of the Bay Line Railroad headquartered in Panama City, Florida, donated the land for the new jail east of downtown Dothan. In the 1990s, Durden had donated both the land and the building that now houses the Dothan Fire Department.

One of the greatest boons to Houston County's economy came in the 1970s with the construction of Alabama Power Company's Farley Nuclear Plant, located near the Chattahoochee River. The massive nuclear facility provides its parent, The Southern Company, not only with saleable electricity, but also with taxes that fund a large percentage of the county's revenue base.

It was a grand day for Dothan and Houston County when Sony Corporation began operating a plant on Highway 84 West. The year was 1977 and the plant remains in production today, providing jobs to hundreds of Wiregrass residents. Currently, this plant is the largest manufacturer of magnetic tape in the world.

Twitchell Corporation began in 1922 as a weaver of webbing for radio cabinets. Its current 325,000-square-foot facility on 34 acres in Dothan produces custom-made textiles for customers around the world.

Houston County serves as "The Hub of the Wiregrass" attracting retail business from surrounding areas. Houston County enjoys the largest sales tax revenue per capita of any county in the state.

Agriculture continues to be a major factor in Houston County's economy. Each year the peanut industry contributes approximately $100 million to the economy of Houston County.

If you look closely, historic structures can sill be found throughout the county. One example, the old Philadelphia Colored School House, is located on Green Frog Road in Gordon. The building is now used as the Gordon New Testament Holiness Church.

In 1961, Troy State University (TSU) opened a center at Ft. Rucker in response to the needs of the military for advanced educational opportunities. TSU expanded into Houston County in the 1970s, first via borrowed classrooms from Wallace Community College, then by opening a campus at the former Houston Hotel in downtown Dothan in 1975. In 1990, Troy State University Dothan opened its current modern campus, pictured above, on Highway 231 North.

Wallace Community College has served Houston and surrounding counties since 1949 when 13 students enrolled in the original sheet metal program. Originally a technical school, WCC became a junior college in 1963 and a comprehensive community college authorized to award associate degrees in 1969. The WCC system has campuses in Eufaula, Ft. Rucker, and Mobile, as well as in Dothan.

Fire destroyed part of the original Flowers Hospital building on West Main Street in Dothan in 1974. With the addition of two cardiologists to its staff in 1975, the hospital erected its current facility at Highway 84 West. It has expanded to include 235 acute-care beds, 165 long-term care beds, 38 outpatient beds, and 4 intensive care units. It is the second-largest employer in Houston County, with 1,500 staff members.

Providing quality healthcare and promoting wellness to those it serves, Southeast Alabama Medical Center opened its Women's Center in April 2003. That same year, the hospital had about 270 physicians on medical staff, 400 beds, and 2,200 employees.

The Willoughby Store, built in 1906, still stands in Crosby, immediately east of the Willoughby House. This store served the farm, sawmill, and turpentine still workers on the Willoughby plantation. The Willoughby family maintains the building for use as the offices for their family farm.

Ashford's depot is a good example of late 19th-century railroad architecture. It was built in 1889 as a combination passenger-freight station at a cost of $4,500. It is one of only three surviving railroad stations along the former Atlantic Coastline Railroad between Montgomery and Bainbridge, Georgia.

In 1898, the Roman Catholic community of Houston County was served as a mission of the Eufaula Diocese by a priest who traveled the poor roads four times per year. In 1914, Catholics built the original Church of St. Columba, a frame structure on the northwest corner of Oates and Main Streets. The current church, shown above, was built in 1963. In 1974, St. Columba opened the Good Shepard Mission to serve Catholics in the Columbia area.

The Mt. Nebo African–American Baptist Church stands south of Alga near the Chattahoochee River on Alabama Highway 95. Interestingly, the church grounds incorporate no cemetery.

Pilgrims Rest Baptist Church (East) was established in 1859 in the Crosby Community, south of Gordon. The original church was a log building. Its replacement, a frame building raised in 1911–1912, was refurbished in 1991. In 2003, it was placed on the Alabama Register of Historic Landmarks. From left to right are Lewis Covington, Alice Jordan, Truett Jordan, Pastor Buford Henderson, and the Columbia Baptist Association's Ken Foley.

The Madrid Methodist Church stands in this 2003 photograph as an example of the beauty and design of rural church architecture. Completed in 1910, the steeple houses a bell imported from Europe that is reportedly one of the largest in the area.

The newest incorporated town in Houston County is Rehobeth, south of Dothan. The new High School is both the capstone of Rehobeth's respected school system and a central feature of the community. Built by the Houston County Board of Education to hold 830 students, the school opened in August of 2003.

A wave of religious revivalism at the end of the Civil War spread Methodism across the Deep South. In south-central Houston County, the Big Creek community organized its Methodist church there in 1865. The current church building, pictured above, testifies to the continued strength of the religious community.

The Wiregrass Museum of Art (WMA), founded in 1988, occupies the former home of the steam turbines that generated power for the Dothan municipal electric utility. WMA has converted the power plant, built in 1913 and listed on the National Register of Historic Places, into five galleries and a large meeting space.

This 10-foot-tall, cast-bronze sculpture by Mobile-based artist Casey Downing is the centerpiece of Dothan's Millennium Park. It depicts the Bible verse, "For I heard them say, Let us go to Dothan" (Genesis 37:17), which inspired city founders in 1885 to change the name of the town from Poplar Head.

This replica of the Statue of Liberty stands at the site of the former Sealey Springs Resort in Cottonwood. When Bob Sealey drilled here for oil in the 1920s, he struck hot mineral water instead. Although he lost his dream of petroleum wealth, he capitalized on his find by building a spa and resort for the thriving "water cure" trade.

This log smoke house still stands in the yard of Mr. and Mrs. Truett Jordan in the Crosby Community. One can almost smell the sausage and ham being cured with hardwood smoke.

The Crosby Post Office building still stands south of Gordon. Abe Crosby was the first postmaster and town namesake. In 1912, the village boasted 50 residents. Later, Crosby moved toward the Chattahoochee River where he established another post office. This one was Lucy, named for his wife.

This is the old single-room brick jail at Gordon in a photograph taken in 2003. Although the age of the structure is unknown, it has been out of service for many years. Standing in the doorway is former Houston County Sheriff Department employee Lewis Covington.

This marker, located on Highway 84 West near Brannon Stand, commemorates the west Houston County home of Rev. Bob Jones, evangelical preacher and founder of Bob Jones University in South Carolina. Jones received his early education at Mallilieu Seminary in Kinsey.

These two gentlemen are part of the extensive African-American community in the southeast section of Houston County. At right is Turner Saffold, a 97-year old retired farmer whose grandfather was born in slavery. At left is Saffold's friend and neighbor, Joseph Melton, 79, also a retired farmer. Both men remember plowing their fields with oxen and supplementing their meager Depression-era diets with wild game and fish from the Chattahoochee River.

Another historic structure that can be seen today is the 1907 Atlantic Coastline passenger station in the "Dixie" area of downtown Dothan. Listed on the National Register of Historic Places, this building will soon be renovated for use by the Wiregrass Transit Authority.

The Fellows House is an excellent example of historical preservation and re-use. It was moved to the Avon Community on Highway 84 East in 1988 from Ashford, where it had been a famous landmark known as the McArthur House. (See page 66.)

Chattahoochee State Park occupies the extreme southeast corner of Houston County, where it continues the long-standing tradition of outdoor recreation. The Civilian Conservation Corps built the original park in the 1930s, but it languished until Rep.John Beasley secured state funds in the 1980s to repair the old dam and to install hookups for recreational vehicles, restrooms, and running water.

The Dothan Botanical Gardens was developed on Headland Road in Kinsey to propagate and display local plants. The non-profit organization that runs the garden is steered by an executive director and a 24-member board of directors.

Landmark Park was created in 1976 by a small group of Dothan citizens who were concerned about preserving the agricultural heritage of Dothan, Houston County, and surrounding areas. The 100-acre facility features several historic structures that have been relocated to the park for the public to enjoy. Pictured driving a jersey wagon is Houston County resident Woody Peters and his wife, Nell.

Landmark Park strives to preserve many of the rural skills and traditions that were once common in Houston County. In 1992, the park was designated as Alabama's official Museum of Agriculture. Shown trimming the hooves of a horse is Howard Roper while Alan Garner looks on.

Visit us at
arcadiapublishing.com

Printed in the USA
CPSIA information can be obtained
at www.ICGtesting.com
LVHW081958171123
764248LV00009B/843